JAGUAR

TALE OF THE CAT

BY JAY SCHLEIFER

Crestwood House
New York

Maxwell Macmillan Canada
Toronto

Maxwell Macmillan International
New York   Oxford   Singapore   Sydney

Crestwood House
Macmillan Publishing Company
866 Third Avenue
New York, NY 10022

Maxwell Macmillan Canada, Inc.
1200 Eglinton Avenue East
Suite 200
Don Mills, Ontario M3C 3N 1

Macmillan Publishing Company is part of the Maxwell Communication Group of Companies.

First Edition
Produced by Twelfth House Productions
Designed by R Studio T

Printed in the United States of America

10 9 8 7 6 5 4 3 2 1

Library of Congress Cataloging-in-Publication Data

Schleifer, Jay.
Jaguar / by Jay Schleifer.—1st ed.
p.   cm.—(Cool classics)
Includes index.
Summary: Traces the history of the British car company that has
been producing some of the fastest machines on the road for over
seventy years.
ISBN 0-89686-814-1
1. Jaguar automobile—History—Juvenile literature.   [1. Jaguar
automobile—History.]   I. Title   II. Series.
TL215.J3S35   1994
629.222'2—dc20   93-10529

CONTENTS

The incredible E-Type. This car's design is over 35 years old.

1 ON THE PROWL

It springs from its garage like a jungle cat, hitting the street on all fours with a rumbling roar. Powerful headlights lead the way as it hunts for open road.

The creature slinks up the freeway ramp. Like a jungle cat, pausing before the attack, it stops at the entrance. Then it digs in and lets loose with a roar. Lesser creatures jump out of the way to give this king of the road some running room.

It will not rest again until dawn.

The "creature" described above is a Jaguar E-Type roadster, one of the most exciting cars ever built. Its two-seat body is a picture of speed and power. First there's the bullet-shaped nose. Then four polished tail pipes rise from under its upturned tail. Its racing-type, six-cylinder engine is a work of art. It gives the car a top speed of close to 150 miles per hour.

But the most amazing fact about the E-Type is that it was designed more than 35 years ago. Although the car was built during the early 1960s, it still looks as modern as any of today's automobiles. The E-Type is amazing for another reason. For a car of its type, it was priced amazingly low.

For more than 70 years, Jaguar Cars Ltd. of England has been using a formula of affordable price and high performance to bring excitement to car lovers everywhere. And that excitement hasn't been limited to sports cars. The company's sedans share the same hot-blooded spirit.

These days, Jaguar cars are produced at a giant factory in Coventry, England. Thousands of skilled workers and powerful, high-tech machines build these great cars. But it wasn't always this way. Years ago, the company didn't even build automobiles. Let's go back to 1922, when the firm began, and see how it was then.

2 FLIGHT OF THE SWALLOWS

Clink…clink…clink. William Walmsley's hammer hit the metal panel again and again. He was building a car body the hard way—by hand. His "factory" was a little brick shed behind his parents' home in Blackpool, England. And the car he was building had only one wheel and no motor. That's because it was a motorcycle **sidecar.** Twenty-nine-year-old Walmsley built those little buggies for a living.

You've probably seen pictures of sidecars. They're the little teardrop-shaped capsules hooked onto the sides of cycles. They're designed to carry from one to three passengers.

Back in the 1920s, sidecars were popular, especially in Europe. So most sidecar makers had all the customers they could handle. But there was a special reason why riders liked Walmsley's sidecars. They were *slick.* While other sidecars looked like a cross between a baby buggy and a living room sofa, Bill Walmsley's were shaped like bullets or torpedoes. They gave a motorcycle a streamlined appearance. And they cost no more than the others. Great looks at a bargain price! That was something to notice.

One motorcycle rider who noticed was young William Lyons, Walmsley's neighbor. Many years later he'd be known as the man who made Jaguar a great car. But at the time, Lyons was just 20 years old. The son of a piano repairman, he'd learned over his teenage years that *his* favorite music came from car or bike motors.

Even though he was barely out of his teens, Bill Lyons had already been hanging around the vehicle business for some time. In his jobs at local dealers he'd sold Sunbeam, Morris, and Rover cars, all famous British makes.

Now, though, Lyons dreamed of starting his own company. And

he thought the sleek vehicles his neighbor made would be the perfect product.

One day he sat down with Walmsley and suggested an agreement: Lyons would provide the business know-how, while Walmsley would provide style and craftsmanship. Together, they hoped to make the elegant Walmsley sidecar the best-selling sidecar in all of England.

As Walmsley listened to Lyons's ideas, he got more and more excited. He was ready to go for it right away.

"No," said Lyons, "we have to wait a few more weeks."

"What do you mean?" asked Walmsley, confused.

"We have to wait a few weeks until my birthday," replied Lyons. "I'm not old enough to apply for a business license. You have to be 21."

On September 4, 1922, Lyons's twenty-first birthday, the company was launched. The two men named their sidecar the Swallow, after a graceful bird. Just as Lyons promised, the company quickly took flight.

Lyons talked the top motorcycle makers into showing off his sidecars right along with their bikes at motorcycle shows. They were happy to do it, since the sidecars often looked better than the bikes!

Soon orders poured in. Before long, the little company had hired "several men and a few lads," as Lyons later put it. And they'd moved from Walmsley's backyard to a real factory building in town. Swallows were flying off the shipping dock in record numbers.

But Lyons realized that the new company would not grow much if it built only sidecars. The real money was in real cars—cars with engines and a full set of wheels. It would cost a lot if the company had to build cars from scratch. The machines needed to build just

7

Swallow sidecars were more streamlined than the others of their time. This is a 1928 model.

an engine cost more than Lyons and Walmsley could afford. There had to be something in between—a way to produce a line of cars without having to build every part that went into them.

Lyons thought long and hard about the problem and finally came up with a brilliant idea. He would take the products his company engineered so successfully—the spectacular-looking body shells—and pop them onto existing **chassis.** He'd turn another company's dull sedan into a snappy sportster by adding a sleek Swallow body.

Luckily for Lyons, one of the large car companies had just built a perfect sedan for this plan. The car, called the Austin Seven, was one of Britain's first inexpensive autos. It was very reliable—and very dull. As soon as Walmsley and Lyons could, they pulled an Austin Seven to their shop. There they worked a magic change.

The original tall, squarish body was unbolted and thrown away. It was replaced with a dashing body with a rounded tail. Much better!

Then Lyons really got creative. He had his workers make the hard metal roof panel removable. That way the owner could have both the openness of a convertible and the weatherproofing of a sedan. The car even included a foldaway soft top for sudden downpours. When the weather was nice, owners simply unbolted the top and left it in the garage.

Finally, Swallow added something else: fun colors. At the time, most British cars were offered in black or dark brown. But you could get your new Swallow sportster in cherry red, Danish blue, light mole brown, cream, and violet. Or, if you were in a military mood, there was battleship gray.

The final touch was a new name on the front of the car—Austin-Swallow.

As with the sidecars, Bill Lyons knew what the market wanted. The Austin-Swallow was a hit! Swallow versions of other British cars followed. Buyers could purchase Morris-Swallows, Swift-Swallows, and Standard-Swallows from Lyons and Walmsley. The Swallow people were now in the car business.

By 1927, just five years after starting the company, Lyons had to change its name. It was now the Swallow Sidecar *and Coachbuilding* Company. He also had to change the factory location. The firm had grown so fast that Lyons couldn't find the skilled workers he needed to build his cars in Blackpool. Blackpool was a beach town where the main business was running hotels. The solution: relocate in a factory town.

After some searching, Lyons chose Coventry, a city in the central part of England. Jaguar is still headquartered there today.

At about the same time, Lyons took another big step. He set up dealers in overseas nations. Swallow was now becoming a seller of car bodies throughout the world.

But Swallow still was not building complete cars. That would be the next step.

3 SWIFT AS THE WIND, SILENT AS A SHADOW!

"The SS is coming! The SS is coming!"

So said the ad in all the major car magazines. It invited car buyers to see the new SS before they ordered their new vehicles. Readers were told that the car would be built by Bill Lyons's Swallow Company. But what did SS stand for?

Most buyers didn't know. And surprisingly, neither did Bill Lyons—or so he said.

But the SS was the car Lyons had dreamed about: Swallow's first original car. It was designed by the company's own engineers.

In truth, the car wasn't completely new. The engine was built by the Standard Company, another British carmaker. But the chassis did come from Swallow. So did the body. And what a body it was...low and sleek, fast and racy.

To buyers, the price was as pretty as the car. It cost just 310 pounds in British money—about $1,000 in the United States. But the car looked much more expensive. Its styling had hints of the costly Bentley luxury cars of the time.

Lyons's ads proudly called the SS "the car with the 1,000 pound look." And that's how it came to be known.

By 1935, Lyons and his company had improved their car so much that they decided to put out a dramatic new model.

The story of the new model begins with the engine. It was partly designed by Harry Weslake, a noted engine tuner of the time. Weslake had started out with a Standard engine that produced 75 horsepower. He wanted to raise that number to 95 horsepower but ended up with 105! That made the new vehicle one of the few affordable cars that broke the magic 100 horsepower barrier.

Lyons thought this achievement deserved a new name. He wanted something that would express the new machine's power and grace, so he sent his secretary to the library for a book on animal names. A list of wild animal names was created. It no longer exists, but we know the name he chose. It was *Jaguar*.

To celebrate the new model, Lyons asked Bill Rankin, a designer of advertising, to create a new emblem. It featured a sleek jungle cat leaping into the air. The same emblem is still used today.

Always the businessman, Lyons had his new car made into a little model. The toy-size Jaguar sold for two **guineas,** about $7.

The new car would be known as the SS100 Jaguar. And the ads had a lot to say about this exciting new machine. "Swift as the wind, silent as a shadow come the SS Jaguars," read one 1935 ad.

The new car got another boost when a letter arrived on Lyons's desk. It was from Captain Sir Malcolm Campbell, who was famous for the speed records he set. A rich sportsman, Campbell had built world speed records in machines for land and water travel. He was the first person to break 300 mph in a car. He set similar records in superfast boats. Now he wrote:

Swallow really took off when the racy SS line appeared. Look at the size of those Lucas headlamps!

I was so impressed with the styling qualities of the new SS Jaguar that I've ordered one from your London agent. Wishing your company continued success.

—M. Campbell

Of course, this letter immediately appeared in an ad, pushing

sales even higher. Jaguar's success went on for four years. But the company changed abruptly on September 1, 1939. That was the day that the world faced the terrible headline:

GERMANY INVADES POLAND

The Second World War had started.

4 WINGS AND WHEELS FOR WAR

SS Cars, Ltd. (which was the company's new name) stopped making private cars almost as soon as World War II began. Everything that the factory produced was needed for the war.

Some of the tools the company made were the same products it had always manufactured. The only difference was that they were now painted army drab. British motorcycle troops rode into battle with the company's sidecars carrying their machine gunners. SS Cars made thousands of smaller trailers to be pulled by army trucks. The company also turned out a few cars for the police and other government agencies. This was the beginning of a long history of supplying police cars.

The major part of the war work, though, involved airplanes. At last, SS products would take to the sky like the swallow they were named after. The company made wings and other parts for Lancaster bombers and the legendary Spitfire fighter.

As it turned out, the city of Coventry was a top German target. And the SS factory was bombed during German raids. Compared with the rest of the city, though, SS had a fairly easy time of it. Damage was relatively light.

In the middle years of the war, the company got a new, top-secret project. SS was asked to build the wings and middle section of an important new plane—a plane *without* propellers! This plane was called the Meteor, one of the world's first jets. SS helped this incredible machine get off the ground.

The Meteor also helped SS. While building the plane, the company learned about **monocoque** (mon-uh-COKE) **construction** (also called *unit construction*). This type of construction replaces a separate frame and body with a single unit. And the single unit is both lighter and stronger. This construction would be used later in Jaguar cars.

The war caused another big change. To pay for new machinery, Lyons had to sell off older parts of the company, including the sidecar business that started it all. As he signed the sale papers, did Lyons think of Bill Walmsley? Bill had left the company some years before, when it was still known as Swallow. Once the sale was final, SS soared ahead!

 ## 5 GREAT LEAP

When the war ended in 1945, car production picked up again at SS Cars. The first cars off the line were designs from before the war. That didn't really matter to customers. They hadn't had the chance to buy new cars during the war. So now they gobbled up anything that came down the road. But Lyons knew that this trend wouldn't last. Soon buyers would want to pick and choose. He had to get going on new models.

First, though, he had to do something about the name of his company and its cars—SS. When Swallow took the name "SS," Hitler and his SS private army, which during the war ran the Nazis' brutal death camps, were not very well known.

By 1945, though, the British people had fought a bloody war against the Germans. They were not going to buy a car called SS, even if it didn't have anything to do with Hitler. Luckily, Lyons had already chosen a name to replace it. Like the 1930s SS models, his cars would be called Jaguars. And his company would be Jaguar Cars Ltd.

Now it was time to turn to that model.

Jaguar had never had a new engine. In fact, it didn't even have an engine of its own. Its power plants had always been built by

The SS100 was the first model to be called a Jaguar. Note how the windshield flips down to reveal racing windscreens.

Jaguar's **XK** engine has powered both street and racing machines for decades.

Standard. But now Lyons decided to build his engine with the money he'd made during the war.

Lyons had a list of requirements for the new car. The new engine had to have at least 160 horsepower. This was a high output for the time and the price of the car. The car also had to be smooth and easy to drive. It had to be built so that it could be easily improved. And it had to be "glamorous," like high-priced cars from Bugatti or Ferrari. Lyons wanted the look and feel of an expensive car, but at a low price.

The first new engine was code-named XA. "X" stood for experimental, and "A" stood for the first engine tried. The next one was called XB.

Jaguar was on the code XF before it found a design that was worth building. And it was on XJ before the engine was really right. These were four-cylinder units. Jag also decided to try a six-cylinder engine, and the final six cylinder was labeled XK. Those two letters would become famous.

The XK engine was a marvel. It was smooth and fast. And it had **dual overhead cams** like a racer. Now it was time to match this engine with a body.

The car Jaguar planned to use the XK in was a family sedan. The British call this kind of car a **saloon.** This new family car would carry Jaguar into a bright future.

But at the last minute, Lyons decided to put a sports car together first. He decided to introduce the sporty model first for two reasons. One, the sports car would get some publicity and prepare the public for the car that really counted—the saloon. Two, if something was wrong with the engine, sports car owners would be less likely to fly off the handle. High-powered machines always needed service, anyway.

Of course, Lyons needed a sports car body design. But he'd

been involved with design since the sidecar days. So he got his skilled metal workers together and told them what he wanted.

As the new car began to take shape, Bill Lyons let his imagination run free. Although other cars of the day were squarish, his new design had almost no straight lines. It was a blend of large and small curves that added up to a totally new look.

A major part of this new look happened because Lyons wrapped all the small parts into the body lines. Until then, everything stuck out. On other cars, headlights stood on their own. Fenders hung off the body. Even the spare tire was bolted on the outside of the trunk.

Lyons's body enclosed all these parts in one "envelope." The lights shone through holes in the front of the car. The spare tire was in the trunk. The fenders were part of the body.

This design provided a smooth overall look. It also let the car cut through the wind better. And it held the price down. One large body shape cost less to build than lots of smaller pieces bolted together.

Naming the car was easy. The engine code "XK" was joined to the car's top speed, 120 miles per hour. And the Jaguar XK-120 prepared to meet the world.

At the 1948 London Auto Show, the public looked and gasped. People could not believe their eyes. A top speed of 120 made the new car one of the fastest factory-produced machines ever. In fact, it may have been *the* fastest. The price of the car surprised people, too. Lyons was selling this incredible machine for about *half* of what similar cars cost.

Magazine writers began to doubt the car. There must be some catch, they wrote. No car could deliver everything the XK-120 promised.

The XK-120's "envelope body" enclosed all the car's parts in one smooth shell.

Lyons had to *prove* his car's greatness. He flew a planeload of reporters to Belgium, where he'd made arrangements to test the cars. Then he hired a racing driver, R. M. V. ("Soapy") Sutton, to put the Jaguar through its paces.

"Soapy was the nervous type," remembered one engineer. Soapy may have suffered from a case of the jitters. But once he got the XK-120 on the road, he produced runs of 132 and 133 mph! And then he ran the car at 10 mph in high gear, a speed that would stall lesser engines. The XK took it all in stride.

When Soapy's antics hit the headlines, orders came rushing in. Everybody wanted the XK-120. Jaguar's new saloon had to play second fiddle to this unplanned, mega-hit sports car.

Many orders came from the United States. During the war, thousands of American soldiers had spent time in England. There they found out how delightful European sports cars could be. Now they wanted to bring that kind of fun home. And there was no better way to do it than in an XK-120. The smooth-lined beast could run rings around just about anything built on this side of the Atlantic!

The success of the XK had another effect on Jaguar. The company had to move to bigger quarters a second time. A factory was built on Browns Lane in Coventry, making that street famous to all car lovers. Don't think it's a muddy cow path, though. It's a major street with a major factory on it!

In time, the XK-120 was improved. The car got a larger engine, better brakes, and even an automatic gearbox. It became known as the XK-140, then the XK-150. In all, the design lasted 13 years. And the wonderful XK engine is still around, powering Jaguars today!

 THE CATS GO RACING

Almost as long as there have been cars, there have been car races. And the slogan "Win on Sunday, sell on Monday!" is a main reason carmakers take part in racing. Cars that win on the track sell better—especially sports cars.

Jaguar had been racing even before the early SS models. But it wasn't until the creation of the XK engine that Jaguar really got into high gear on the race track. To get into big-time racing, Jaguar took the XK-120 and made minor improvements. The engines that Jaguar designers created were fast and durable. But they were no match for the racing machines that Ferrari, Mercedes-Benz, and others had built for top events. Jaguar knew it had to build a special race car engine if it really wanted to win big races.

The first race car Jaguar built was the powerful XK-120C, or C-Type, as it was later known. (The "C" stood for "competition.") Jaguar engineers created a lightweight frame, made of thin, but strong, steel tubes, around the basic XK engine. The tubes were arranged in triangles, the strongest shape known. Then body panels were welded to the tubes to add more strength.

This frame was covered with a special racing body, which had been tested for streamlining in a wind tunnel. Under the body, steering and brakes had been improved. And a whole new rear end had been designed.

The car looked good. But how would it run?

"Lofty" England would find out. A longtime Jaguar employee, Lofty had been named what he called "the sort of unofficial Competition Manager."

Lofty hired driver Peter Walker to check the new car out. Round and round the track Walker went. As he did, Lofty became more and more disappointed. Walker couldn't seem to reach the speeds Lofty knew the car was capable of.

Finally, Lofty called his driver in for a little chat.

"I looked at Walker," said Lofty, "and I noticed that he had some strangely tinted goggles on." So Lofty told the driver to put some clear goggles on and try it again. Walker went back to the track and broke the lap record.

It's hard to find a straight line on this gorgeous XK roadster!

Jaguar knew it had a car that could run with the best racing machines. But would it last like the best of them? This question was vital because the British planned on entering Europe's top long-distance races. These included the 1,000-mile Mille Miglia in Italy and France's 24-hour race at Le Mans.

The C-Type's first major test was the 1951 Le Mans. The engineers at Jaguar had a good feeling going into the race. This was because a stock XK-120 car had lasted 21 hours the year before. And that car was not even designed for the grueling pace of the Le Mans.

Now the C-Jags went out and began to show the competition what British cars could do. Three Jaguars were entered. From the beginning, they were the fastest cars on the track. One dropped out because of a broken part. But the other two raced to the finish, and one won the race!

In its first try, the magical C-Type had been the winner of one of the world's top races. It was the first of many Le Mans victories.

 ## JAGUAR GETS THE BRAKES

Shocked by the British victory, the other teams reacted for the 1952 season. Ferrari and other makers added a lot of improvements to their cars. They hoped to send the former sidecar maker back to England—on the trailer! But Jaguar had an even bigger surprise to spring in the 1952 season—a secret weapon.

The new company from Browns Lane was about to introduce the world's first practical automotive **disk brakes.**

Until then, almost all car brakes worked pretty much the way they had in the days of the Model T Ford. They were called **drum**

brakes. They featured moving parts inside a closed drum that was attached to the wheels. When the driver pushed the brake pedal, the parts pressed against the inside of the drum. This slowed the drum and the wheel attached to it.

The design was simple, and it worked. But it had flaws. On rainy days water splashed into the drum and made the parts slip. Also, when brakes are used hard, they create a lot of heat. The heat gets trapped inside the drums. This warped the parts and weakened the brakes.

Disk brakes work like the brakes on a 10-speed bicycle. Fingerlike grippers grab and squeeze the wheel from both sides until it stops. The only real difference is that on a car, the grippers grab a disk that's attached to the wheel instead of grabbing the wheel itself. Since there is no closed drum, water can spin away from the brakes. And excess heat doesn't get trapped. The brakes stay drier and cooler, and they work better.

The new brakes were first used in the 1952 Mille Miglia. This was a killer race if ever there was one! Superstar driver Stirling Moss was at the wheel of the disk brake-equipped C-Type car.

One of his competitors was Rudi Caracciola (Kar-rah-SEE-oh-lah), an ace on the Mercedes-Benz team. Rudi was driving a bigger, more powerful car than the Jag.

"We caught up with him," said Moss, "and for about 60–70 miles, we were able to outbrake him every time! He'd start to slow for a corner, and expect us to do the same, but we went by him flat out, then put the brakes on in front of him. He said it was incredible! Several times, he didn't think the car was going to stop!"

It stopped. And it won—and won and won! Though engine cooling problems cost Jaguar the Le Mans in 1952, the team took the 1953 race. The company had won two Le Mans victories in only three years.

The C-Type racer was Jaguar's first all-out racing machine. It won Le Mans on its first try!

C-Types brought disk brakes to racing. Ferraris could go just as fast, but couldn't stop as quickly.

But Jaguar excitement was just beginning. An even more potent weapon was already on the drawing board back in Coventry— the legendary D-Type.

 "D" FOR DOMINATION

Ask a champion what's wrong with being top gun in a sport. You'll probably get this answer—everybody else comes gunning for you. That's just what happened to Jaguar with the success of the C-Type.

Within a year Mercedes-Benz had built the 300SLR, perhaps

the finest all-around racer in auto history. Ferrari and Maserati also had new models. Even Chevrolet was making an entry, with a sleek machine called the Corvette.

Jaguar knew it would need more than its disk brakes to keep winning. Others would copy that trick. Luckily, the engineers from Browns Lane had another idea: use the air itself to help them win.

Until the 1950s not much attention had been paid to the science called **aerodynamics**—the study of the way air flows over an object like a car's body. But the ability to move smoothly through the wind was important at tracks such as Le Mans.

At this kind of track, a single straightaway could be 3 miles long. Cars could reach speeds of over 170 mph! At such speeds, the ability to cut through wind might give a driver the needed edge. Sometimes this was more important than an engine's power. A smoothly shaped car could actually go faster than a more powerful machine of less streamlined design.

Jaguar studied streamlining. The company hired Malcolm Sayer, a noted expert in the field, to design the body of the new racer. It was called the D-Type. The result was an incredibly smooth machine that took ideas from both aircraft and automobile design.

The D's body was a flowing wave of metal. It started with a sleek, scooped nose and ended in a smooth, rounded tail. Nothing stuck out. Nothing disturbed the airflow. The car also had a single high-flying fin behind the driver's head. The fin acted like an airplane's tail to make the car more stable.

The amazing D-Type reached top speeds that were unheard of in sports car racing. The car came alive at 170 mph. The faster the pace, the better the D liked it. Top speed was above 190.

The car was definitely streamlined. But it was fast for another reason. It was built like the Meteor jets that Swallow had built

Jaguar engineers created an incredibly streamlined machine in the D-Type. This car knocked on the 200 mph door!

during the war. These jets had one body unit that replaced both the body and the frame. The result was a light, strong vehicle.

Now the D received this kind of construction, the monocoque structure. This was added to its bulletproof XK engine, which had been improved. It now had triple carbs and 275 horsepower, improved suspension, and, of course, disk brakes.

With the monocoque construction and the improved engine, the D car was amazing! The *D* in the car's name could have stood for domination. That's what the car was capable of. And it definitely dominated at some of the world's top racetracks. Some racers probably thought that the only way to beat the D-Jag was to cheat!

Some Jaguar fans say that's just what happened at the 1954 Le Mans race. And nearly 50 years later, they're still mad. The new cars ran like clockwork demons as the race began. But they suddenly went into coughing fits all over the track. All three D-types were called in to find what the problem was.

The crews found a fine gray sand in the fuel. It was clogging everything in sight!

The suspicious thing was that all cars in the race got their fuel from the same supply. But only the Jags had the problem. Had the Jags been sabotaged? Did some frustrated fan of another brand seek to do them in? We'll never know.

What we do know is that the mechanics cleaned out the engines. Then the drivers began a desperate chase to gain the lead. Lap after lap, Jaguar drivers let it all hang out. They gained on the leading Ferraris with every lap. But time proved the enemy. Twenty-four hours were not enough to catch up. At the end of the long event, the first Jag crossed the finish line just 105 *seconds* behind the winning Ferrari.

A disappointed English team saddled up for the trip home, hoping that the 1955 race would end differently.

It did, but in an unfortunate way. In one of the great tragedies of racing, a speeding Mercedes-Benz flipped into the crowd, killing scores of people. Mercedes pulled out of the race, leaving Jaguar to win. It was not the kind of victory anyone wanted, but it did make for three Le Mans trophies in five years.

The 1956 race continued the string of victories as a privately entered D-Jag took the checkered flag. The D-Type won again in 1957. The 1957 race was the D's last victory at Le Mans, but it was also its greatest. Five cars were entered, and four finished—in first, second, fourth, and sixth spots. This Jaguar parade made a total of five wins in seven years. No other car matched this record at Le Mans for many years afterward.

The Big Cats of Coventry had brought fame, fortune, and honor to their company, city, and nation. To help celebrate, Queen Elizabeth of England made an official visit to the Jaguar plant late in 1956. Her Majesty paraded up and down the assembly line with ministers in tow. She cast her regal glow over the parts department. She even royally checked out the doings under a D-Type's flip-up engine cover.

That same year the queen also awarded Bill Lyons a special honor. For all of his hard work and success with Jaguar, Lyons was made a knight. Henceforth and forever, this man from Blackpool would be addressed as Sir William Lyons. Hip, hip, hooray!

But surprisingly, at the peak of its fame, the factory also had an announcement. It was pulling out of racing. The time and energy of the engineers were needed for another special project.

 9   **THE EXCELLENT "E"**

The "project" that pulled the plug on racing was Jaguar's first totally new sports car since the XK-120, which had first appeared in 1948.

The XK was produced for a decade. And though it had been upgraded twice—as the XK-140 and XK-150—everyone agreed it was getting old. New sports cars from Italy, France, and even the U.S. (the new Corvette) were taking sales away from Jaguar.

Work on the new car began in 1957, just as the D-Jags were finishing their run of racing victories. The first design decision was to keep the XK engine. This engine had made Jaguar great. It had been tuned in the D-Type for more than 250 horsepower, and that was all the new car would need.

Sir William Lyons and his pride and joy, the E-Type. You can see the D-Type racer's lines in the bullet nose and oval grille.

For the body, Lyons and his engineers again turned to what had worked so well for the D. The new car would be designed by the streamlining specialist Malcolm Sayer, who had worked on the D. And it would be built with the same kind of light but strong monocoque structure. Small frames were attached to the front and rear to carry the engine and the suspension parts.

The front suspension was pretty much as it had been on previous Jags. But the rear end did the D-Jag one better! The new E-Type would include Jaguar's first production **independent rear suspension. IRS,** as it's known, features each rear wheel mounted separately to the frame. That way, if a bump lifts one wheel, the other is not affected.

In the D and the old XK autos, the wheels were connected by a stiff metal post called a **beam axle.** When one wheel jumped, so did the other. And the car's handling could be upset right in the middle of a turn.

But all of this great engineering in the new E-Type paled in comparison with the car's looks. Sayer, with plenty of input from Sir William Lyons, had created a masterpiece. Many car lovers still consider the E-Jag to be the best-looking sports car of all time.

To understand how advanced the E-Type's design was, you have to consider the other cars of the 1950s and early 1960s.

American models were huge boxes covered with **chrome** trim and tail fins. European cars were mostly squared and old-fashioned-looking. Sports cars were barely catching up to what Jaguar had done years earlier with the XK-120. Britain's MG and Triumph had only recently given up separate, stand-up headlights and fenders. They now used an envelope body like the 120.

Jaguar's new design featured a long, clean, bullet-shaped body even sleeker than that of the D-Type racer. The nose was simple and rounded. An oval slot let air into the engine and brakes. The hood section was covered with cooling slots, which gave a racing

The E-Type's nose flipped up to reveal the XK engine. Those two long shapes are overhead cam units.

touch. And like the D-Jag's, the engine cover opened like a clamshell to make the engine easy to work on.

Out back, the rear was simple, flat, and rounded. Taken as a whole, the car looked a lot like a jet airplane, without the wings and tail. And shiny wire wheels and bladelike bumpers let the basic shape shine through.

Two versions of the car were built. One was an open roadster, which the British call a **drop head.** The other was a closed coupe, which is called a **fixed head.** The coupe was even sleeker than the open car. It had a rounded top that sloped back to the rear in an egg shape. Like any egg, this one had a hatch—a hatchback that opened to reveal the luggage area.

Under the flip hood, the XK engine gleamed like a jeweled ring in a velvet box. Many thought the sight of it alone was worth the price of the car.

As to that price, Lyons again stunned the car world. The new Jaguar would sell for just about $4,200. That was about the price of a Cadillac. It wasn't cheap, but it was nowhere near the price of a Ferrari or a top-of-the-line Mercedes.

The new Jaguar had both show and go. The E-Type's top speed was close to 150 mph, right out of the dealer's showroom! Zero to 60 miles per hour came in under seven seconds. And with Jag's disk brakes at all four wheels, the car stopped even more quickly than it gained speed. Gas mileage was pretty good, too. The car got 15 to 20 miles per gallon.

As with the XK-120, Sir William Lyons had created a genuine bargain. It was a great car at a truly affordable price. If they could have, sports car lovers would have knighted him all over again!

The E-Type first appeared at the Geneva Auto Show in Switzerland in 1961. It was featured as the cover car on auto magazines worldwide. And as soon as the world got a glimpse of the new Jag, orders poured into the now rebuilt Browns Lane factory.

Over the next 14 years, the car was improved. A larger XK engine was fitted, bringing the engine size from the original 3.8 liters up to 4.2 liters. A four-seat version was added in 1966. It somehow kept the beautiful lines, even with a longer body and taller top. And then, in the 1970s, Jaguar fitted the car with the company's first V-12 engine. It was a marvelously smooth power plant—as high-tech as anything from Ferrari or Lamborghini. But, of course, it cost less.

Eventually, E-Type production ended to make way for other models. The date the last E car rolled off the assembly line was February 1975. Some 72,520 of the sleek cats had been built.

10 THE FASTEST SALOONS IN THE WEST

Americans love Jaguar for its sleek sports and racing cars. But the English know Jaguar in another way, as a major producer of *family* cars. Ever since the first Austin-Swallows, family saloons have been part of the company's line.

In the British market, Jaguar is a mid-priced car. It's more costly than the small Austin, Morris, and Vauxhall models that are similar to our Ford, Chevy, and Plymouth cars. But the Jaguar price doesn't come close to Rolls-Royce or Bentley luxury cars.

The XJ-6 and XJ-12 are two saloons that Jaguar has sold in America. You may have seen these sleek machines on the streets of large cities, where they are as classy as a BMW, Lexus, or Mercedes. But there are other Jaguar models that aren't sold in the United States.

Jaguar's saloon cars are often used by Britain's police forces. Officers love the speed and great handling of their cats. And the thought of a police Jag with lights flashing and European *EEE-AWW-EEE-AWW* siren blasting strikes fear into criminals all over Britain. **Scotland Yard** has a fleet of the vehicles. And if fictional detective Sherlock Holmes were alive today, his **carriage** would probably be a Jaguar.

Another Jag familiar to Americans is the XJ-S Grand Touring, or GT machine. This large four-seat coupe replaced the E-Type in the mid-1970s and is still sold in the 1990s. It's the Jag you're most likely to see on the streets today.

Powered by either an XK or later 6-cylinder, or Jaguar's V-12, the XJ-S is not really a sports car, as the E-Type was. But Jaguar felt it needed a car with more sales appeal than a two-seater. And

British police often drive Jaguar cars. Here, one
Jaguar has been caught by another!

buyers have proven them right. The XJ-S has done well in the market.

Jaguar lovers, though, have long wondered when their favorite company will again build a true sportster—the mythical "F-Type." Rumors about this car have come up again and again. "The factory is working on it." Then, "The project has been dropped." And, a few months later, "It's back again."

As this book was written, there was no official F-Type. Nor were there plans for one. But Jaguar fans remain on the alert for any sign of one. And we wish them luck.

11 RETURN OF THE RACING CATS

When Jaguar parked the D-Type in 1957, it seemed that the company had written off racing for good. But just five years later, modified E-Types began showing up at races all over Europe. Apparently the big cats just couldn't stay away from the track.

There was, however, a big difference between showing up and winning. Just as with the XK-120s, there was no way E-Types, even when modified for racing, could keep up with the specially built racers of companies like Ferrari or Porsche. Jaguar fans pleaded with the factory to build such a car and get back into big-time racing.

The first sign of that happening came in the 1970s, when a two-factory racing team jumped into the action. Group 44 Racing was a United States team that started by driving E-Types. Later, the team raced the XJR-5. It was state of the art, with a V-12 Jag engine mounted in a chassis made of **honeycomb construction.** Honeycomb looks just like its namesake—the inside of a beehive. It consists of six-sided metal chambers. The result is lightness combined with great strength.

Then, in the 1980s, another racing team started up in Britain. It was called Tom Walkinshaw Racing, or TWR. This team began entering XJSs in sedan races. But it wasn't long before it moved on to build new racers, with factory help.

TWR's car, the XJR-6, was even more advanced than the XJE-S. The underside of the car directed air and created a vacuum-cleaner effect. The car was "sucked" down against the road so it stuck like glue on turns. This method of using airflow to improve handling is called **ground effects**.

Both the Group 44 and TWR machines were genuine long-distance racers. Able to reach 200 mph, they were suited for racetracks like Le Mans. Many people think that helping these teams was really Jaguar's way to return to Le Mans.

But in the years since the D-Type, the famous French race had become a Porsche playground. The German cars won like clockwork almost every year. Jag had to work its way back into the winner's circle.

That took a full four years, with more and more advanced and competitive cars each year. The XJR series got up to XJR-9 before a Jaguar saw the victorious checkered flag at Le Mans, in 1988.

The race was a tremendous duel. After 24 hours of racing, the winning cat finished just two minutes ahead of the best-running Porsche.

Though there have been other important victories since, this was the big one. After a 30-year dry spell, the big cats had again proven their power and glory on the world's top track!

12 THE SATURDAY CLUB AND THE SUPER JAG

With a win at Le Mans, Jaguar was again top dog on the track. But what about the road? Would Ferrari, Porsche, and Lamborghini run rings around Jaguar out where the customers lived?

Not if a small group of Jaguar employees had its way. This was the "Saturday Club."

The club began in the mid-1980s, when the private teams were just beginning their victorious ride. At the time, supercars were the rage. And Jaguar learned that two of its rivals, Ferrari and

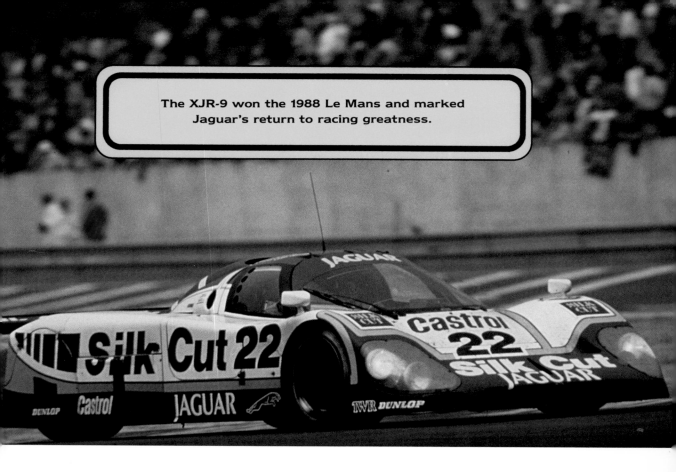

The XJR-9 won the 1988 Le Mans and marked
Jaguar's return to racing greatness.

Porsche, were planning new high-performance cars. Those cars
became the Ferrari F40 and the Porsche 959. Jaguar engineers
desperately wanted their company to build a Super Jaguar that
would dazzle the competition.

Jaguar managers wanted to make their engineers happy. And
they wanted to keep their company on the cutting edge. So the
managers okayed work on such a car if the engineers were willing
to do it on their own time—on *Saturdays,* for example.

It took a lot Saturdays, and a lot of begged and borrowed parts.
But the result was worth it. One day the leanest, meanest, most rip-
roaring Jaguar ever built for the road sat on the builder's stand.

The new Super Cat would, in final form, have a 500-plus   **43** horsepower, twin-**turbo** engine. It would also have a racing-designed frame and body, and ground-effects streamlining. Yet it also sported a full leather interior and air-conditioning.

It was a ground-level executive jet, built to do zero to 60 in four seconds, and zero to 100 in eight. Its top speed was a breathtaking 220 mph!

To name their beast, the engineers looked back in Jaguar history. Another famous Jag, the XK-120, had gotten its number to match its top speed. So the new car became the XJ-220.

Jaguar knew that such a car would need to be built by hand. It wasn't a job for their fast-moving factory. So TWR was called in. Jaguar then joined with the racing specialists to create a new company called JaguarSport. The company would build the XJ-220 for the street. And to keep the car valuable for collectors, only 350 of the monsters would be produced before the line shut down.

Each car would carry a monstrous price tag—higher than half a million dollars! What's more, would-be owners had to make a down payment of nearly one hundred thousand dollars. This was just to reserve their car! The vehicles wouldn't be delivered for years.

Even at those terms, the sales book was full within weeks of XJ-220's announcement. Long before the first car was built, the Super Jag was a sellout!

After several delays, the first XJ-220s began to roll out in 1992. Test drivers were thrilled, although some adjustments were needed to make the car perfect.

"At 200 mph, you have to add a little steering," said test driver Davy Jones. "And at 210, I thought the car was getting a bit light when it hit a bump. But considering the speed, I thought it settled down rather quickly."

More quickly than its driver, most likely!

Anything else, Davy?

"Being a test model, it didn't have full sound deadening," he said. "The easy fix is to turn up the stereo. Eric Clapton would do nicely."

13 THE FUTURE OF JAGUAR

As the 1990s began, Jaguar was doing well.

The company had solved most of its business problems. It had returned to racing. It was selling exciting new models. And, in the XJ-220, the company even had a Super Cat to hold its banner high. Then there was a sudden announcement that stunned car lovers everywhere: *Jaguar had been sold, lock, stock, and steering wheels, to the Ford Motor Company!*

Nightmares of Jags that looked like overstuffed, vinyl-roofed cars began to haunt fans.

Not to worry. We know Ford by its American cars. But, in fact, Ford has long owned car factories worldwide. It lets each of them do its own thing. There is little in common between the cars produced by Ford of England and the American models. And that's how it's expected to be at Jaguar. You'll never mistake the new F-Type (if it's ever built) for your neighbor's T-Bird.

As for Jaguar, look for the company to continue to build some of the world's most exciting cars—sedans, GTs, and sportsters. And look for more racing. It's part of the company's history and **heritage**.

In fact, you can expect the 70-year-old Cool Classic cat from Britain to keep getting better and better!

 GLOSSARY/INDEX

aerodynamics 31   The study of how air flows over an object like a vehicle; streamlining.

beam axle 36   Solid metal bar connecting two rear wheels of a car. It is cheap and easy to build but can cause both rear wheels to jump when one hits a bump.

carriage 39   British slang for car.

chassis 8, 10   The frame and major mechanical parts of a car, including the engine, transmission, and suspension.

The XJ-220 "Super-Jag"...what you can do on Saturdays if you *really* put your mind to it!

chrome 36 A metal that shines like a mirror. It is used to decorate car bodies.

disk brakes 26, 27, 31, 32, 38 A stopping system that works by pressing on a spinning disk attached to a wheel. Disk brakes are especially good in wet weather.

drop head 37 The British term for a convertible car or open roadster.

drum brakes 26, 27 A stopping system that works by pressing on the inside of a closed drum attached to a wheel. In wet weather, drum brakes tend to hold wetness inside, cutting stopping power.

47

dual overhead cams 19 A system for quickly opening and closing engine valves, allowing an engine to breathe better and produce more power.

fixed head 37 The British term for a closed coupe.

ground effects 41, 44 The shaping of the underside of a car body to cause a vacuum, "sticking" the car to the ground for better handling in turns and at high speeds. It is used in many racing designs.

guinea 11 British money term meaning a pound and a shilling; about $3–4 in U.S. money.

heritage 45 The history and background of a person, company, or product such as a make of car.

honeycomb construction 41 A lightweight, strong means of making a car part such as a body. It uses the same "cell" system seen in beehives.

independent rear suspension (IRS) 36 Method of mounting wheels separately to a car chassis so that when one rear wheel hits a bump and moves, the other is not affected. IRS usually provides better handling.

monocoque construction 14, 32, 36 Use of a car body that also acts as a frame. Eliminating a separate frame cuts weight. Most airplanes use this system. Also known as *unit construction*.

saloon 19, 22, 39 British term for sedan or family car.

Scotland Yard 39 British police headquarters, located in London.

sidecar 6, 7, 9, 14, 15, 26 Small, one-wheeled passenger capsule attached to the side of a motorcycle.

turbo 44 Short for turbocharger; a spinning, pumplike device that forces extra gas-air mixture into an engine, creating extra power. A turbocharger is spun by the force of hot exhaust gas rushing through it.